THE PHILOSOPHY OF PLOTINUS